D1516744

PEOPLE OF CHARACTER

Martin Luther King, Jr.

A Life of Fairness

Written by Tonya Leslie
Illustrated by Tina Walski

BELLWETHER MEDIA · MINNEAPOLIS, MN

Note to Librarians, Teachers, and Parents:

Blastoff! Readers are carefully developed by literacy experts and combine standards-based content with developmentally-appropriate text.

Level 1 provides the most support through repetition of high-frequency words, light text, predictable sentence patterns, and strong visual support.

Level 2 offers early readers a bit more challenge through varied simple sentences, increased text load, and less repetition of high frequency words.

Level 3 advances early-fluent readers toward fluency through increased text and concept load, less reliance on visuals, longer sentences, and more literary language.

Level 4 builds reading stamina by providing more text per page, increased use of punctuation, greater variation in sentence patterns, and increasingly challenging vocabulary.

Level 5 encourages children to move from "learning to read" to "reading to learn" by providing even more text, varied writing styles, and less familiar topics.

Whichever book is right for your reader, Blastoff! Readers are the perfect books to build confidence and encourage a love of reading that will last a lifetime!

This edition first published in 2008 by Bellwether Media.

No part of this publication may be reproduced in whole or in part without written permission of the publisher. For information regarding permission, write to Bellwether Media Inc., Attention: Permissions Department, Post Office Box 1C, Minnetonka, MN 55345-9998.

Library of Congress Cataloging-in-Publication Data
Leslie, Tonya.
  Martin Luther King, Jr. : a life of fairness / by Tonya Leslie.
    p. cm. — (People of character) (Blastoff! readers)
Summary: "People of character explores important character traits through the lives of famous historical figures. Martin Luther King, Jr. highlights how this great individual demonstrated fairness during his life. Intended for grades three through six"—Provided by publisher.
  Includes bibliographical references and index.
  ISBN-13: 978-1-60014-090-7 (hardcover : alk. paper)
  ISBN-10: 1-60014-090-4 (hardcover : alk. paper)
  1. King, Martin Luther, Jr., 1929-1968—Juvenile literature. 2. Fairness—Juvenile literature. 3. African Americans—Biography—Juvenile literature. 4. Civil rights workers—United States—Biography—Juvenile literature. 5. Baptists—United States—Clergy—Biography—Juvenile literature. 6. African Americans—Civil rights—History—20th century—Juvenile literature. I. Title.

  E185.97.K5R87 2008
  323.092—dc22
  [B]   2007014945

Contents

You have probably heard
of Martin Luther King, Jr.
There is a street or school
named for him in almost
every state in the country.
There is even a holiday
named after him. But do you
know why he is famous?

Martin Luther King, Jr. was born on January 15, 1929, in Atlanta, Georgia. At that time, African-Americans didn't have the same **rights** as white people. They could not eat in the same restaurants as whites or go to the same schools. This didn't stop Martin. He went to **segregated** schools and got many degrees. He loved to learn.

After his schooling, Martin became a pastor at a church in Montgomery, Alabama. He began to speak about fairness for black people.

He told people to take a stand against **racism**. People were moved by his powerful words and he was asked to speak to groups all around Montgomery.

One day Martin heard about Rosa Parks. Rosa was arrested for not giving her seat to a white person on a bus in Montgomery.

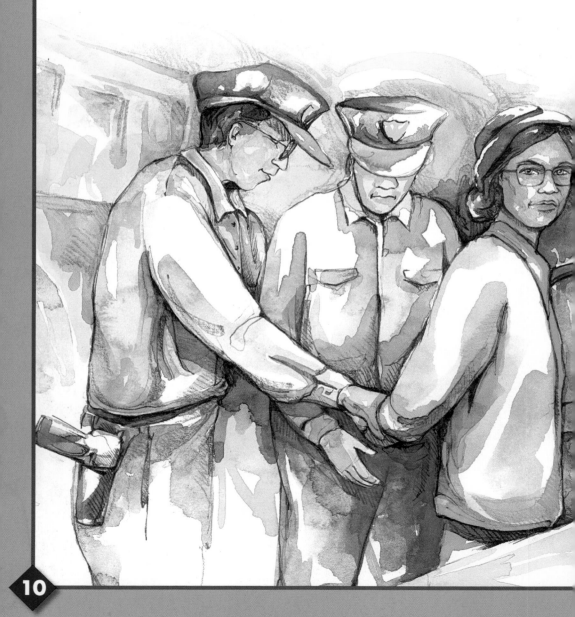

This act set off a **boycott**. African-American people in Montgomery wouldn't ride the buses until laws changed. They needed someone to lead them in **protest**.

Martin was chosen to lead the protest. He encouraged the protestors to fight for their rights. He told them the best weapons were words and peaceful actions. After a year, the laws were changed and the bus boycott finally ended.

Martin was seen as a hero. His powerful words had brought change. This was the start of the **Civil Rights Movement**.

The Civil Rights Movement was a time when many black people fought for equal rights. Martin always encouraged people to protest in peaceful ways. For example, when black people were told they couldn't eat at the same restaurant as white people, they held a **sit-in**.

Protesters filled the seats of the restaurant. They wouldn't leave even though people shouted and threw things at them. These types of quiet protests got the world's attention. Martin was always leading the way.

Martin protested peacefully, but many
people were violent towards him.
His words about fairness angered them.

His home was bombed. He was beaten. He was attacked by dogs. Some of the people who marched with him were hurt and even killed. It was a scary time.

Martin never became violent. He **inspired** people with his wise and peaceful words. He went to **Washington, D.C.** to speak for equal rights. A half million people gathered to hear him speak. He told them about his dream that one day America would be a place where all people were treated fairly.

He imagined a day when no one would be judged by the color of his or her skin. People cheered for his dream.

Martin was awarded a **Nobel Peace Prize** that recognized his work for peace. Many people believed in Martin's dream. Others did not. They wanted things to stay the same. Martin was killed on April 4th, 1968. His powerful voice was silenced. Still, the Civil Rights Movement moved on and more laws were changed.

Many people say Martin's powerful words won the movement.

Martin spoke out for fairness. He fought for change with words instead of violence. Today, people still remember Martin. How do you remember him?

Glossary

boycott—when people refuse to buy goods or a service to force a change

Civil Rights Movement—a national effort led by black people in the United States in the 1950s and 1960s to establish equal rights

inspired—made people want to do something by showing them a good example

Nobel Peace Prize—a famous prize awarded every year to the person who has done the most to help make the world peaceful

protest—to express disapproval

racism—the belief that certain races of people are superior to other races of people

rights—something a person deserves to have

segregated—separated by race

sit-in—a protest in which the protestors peacefully occupy seats typically not available to them

Washington, D.C.—the capital city of the United States of America; D.C. stands for District of Columbia, the area of land that makes up the city.

To Learn More

AT THE LIBRARY

King, Coretta Scott. *My Life with Martin Luther King, Jr.* New York: Holt, Rinehart, and Winston, 1969.

Marzollo, Jean. *Happy Birthday Martin Luther King.* New York: Scholastic, 1993.

Myers, Walter Dean. *I've Seen the Promised Land: The Life of Dr. Martin Luther King, Jr.* New York: HarperCollins, 2003.

Rappaport, Doreen. *Martin's Big Words: The Life of Martin Luther King Jr.* New York: Hyperion Books, 2001.

Ringgold, Faith. *If a Bus Could Talk: The Story of Rosa Parks.* New York: Simon and Schuster, 1999.

ON THE WEB
Learning more about Martin Luther King, Jr. is as easy as 1, 2, 3.

1. Go to www.factsurfer.com

2. Enter "Martin Luther King, Jr." into search box.

3. Click the "Surf" button and you will see a list of related web sites.

With factsurfer.com, finding more information is just a click away.

Index